M000032332

UNDERSTANDING
BIPOLAR
DISORDER

by Kathy MacMillan

BrightP◆int Press

San Diego, CA

BrightP◇int Press

© 2021 BrightPoint Press
an imprint of ReferencePoint Press, Inc.
Printed in the United States

For more information, contact:
BrightPoint Press
PO Box 27779
San Diego, CA 92198
www.BrightPointPress.com

Content Consultant: Lisa T. Eyler, PhD, Professor in Residence, Psychiatry, University of California San Diego

LIBRARY OF CONGRESS CATALOGING-IN-PUBLICATION DATA

Names: MacMillan, Kathy, 1975- author.
Title: Understanding bipolar disorder / by Kathy MacMillan.
Description: San Diego : ReferencePoint Press, [2021] | Series: Mental health guides |
    Includes bibliographical references and index. | Audience: Grades 10-12
Identifiers: LCCN 2020002442 (print) | LCCN 2020002443 (eBook) | ISBN 9781682829851
    (hardcover) | ISBN 9781682829868 (eBook)
Subjects: LCSH: Manic-depressive illness--Juvenile literature.
Classification: LCC RC516 .M312 2021 (print) | LCC RC516 (eBook) | DDC 616.89/5--dc23
LC record available at https://lccn.loc.gov/2020002442
LC eBook record available at https://lccn.loc.gov/2020002443

CONTENTS

AT A GLANCE

- Bipolar disorder (BD) is a mental illness. It causes extreme mood changes.

- People with BD experience two main types of mood episodes. These are manic and depressive episodes. People have a lot of energy during a manic episode. They may do dangerous or unhealthy things. They do not think about risks. During a depressive episode, people have little energy. They feel sad and tired.

- BD affects people's daily lives. It can make it difficult for people to take care of themselves.

- There is no cure for BD. It can be treated to manage symptoms. But it does not go away.

- BD is a complex disease. It has many potential causes. Each person has a different mix of symptoms.

- About 2.8 percent of US adults have symptoms of BD each year. The average age when people first notice symptoms is twenty-five years old.

- About 83 percent of people with BD have severe symptoms.

- There are many successful treatments for BD. They include medication and therapy.

A LIFE OF UPS AND DOWNS

Singer and actress Demi Lovato seemed to have it all. As a teenager, she became famous. She made two successful pop albums. She starred in a Disney Channel television show.

But success wasn't easy. Demi felt like she had to be perfect. Sometimes she stayed up all night writing songs. At other

Demi Lovato has written songs about her struggles with mental illness.

times, she got very sad. She slept all day

long. She dealt with her pain by drinking

alcohol. She also used drugs. Sometimes

she hurt herself. She developed a serious

Demi Lovato first went into treatment in 2010. Today, she continues to perform and write music.

illness called bulimia. Bulimia is a type of

eating **disorder**. She ate large amounts of

food. Then she forced herself to throw up.

Other people had trouble being around

Demi. She yelled a lot. When she was

eighteen years old, she punched a backup dancer. Her friends and family helped her find a treatment program. Demi entered the program to help her stop using drugs. Doctors there also **diagnosed** Demi with bipolar disorder (BD). BD is a mental illness. It causes wild mood swings. Demi was relieved to have an answer. She said, "In a way I knew that it wasn't my fault anymore. Something was actually off with me."[1]

After treatment, Demi seemed to get better. But she still struggled. She took drugs and drank alcohol in secret. Demi decided to be honest. She shared her

Living with BD is difficult, but treatment can help people manage the symptoms.

struggles with mental illnesses. She wanted others who were struggling to know they were not alone.

In 2018, Demi almost died from a drug overdose. She was in the hospital for a long time. It was hard for her to return to work, but she did. She wanted people to see beyond her BD. She said, "It's something that I have, it's not who I am."[2]

Demi's story is not unusual. Millions of people around the world have BD. Sometimes they have a lot of energy. They are excited. At other times, they have little or no energy. They may use drugs, alcohol, or food to try to feel better.

BD can make people feel out of control. But the disorder is treatable. Just like Demi, people with BD can live happy lives with the right treatment.

CHAPTER ONE

WHAT IS BIPOLAR DISORDER?

Most people feel sad when something bad happens. They feel happy when something good happens. These are emotions. They last for a short time. Moods last much longer. A mood is an overall feeling. It is not a reaction to a certain situation. A mood may last for hours or days. Moods affect how people

People with BD may have difficulty controlling their emotions.

feel about the things that happen to them.

People who are in a bad mood are more

likely to feel emotions such as anger and

sadness. They might feel bad even if

something good happens to them.

People who have BD may sometimes ignore loved ones or push them away. This can strain their relationships.

Most people have periods of time when they feel sad or tired. They also have periods when they feel happy and excited. These moods do not last long in people who do not have BD. They do not interfere with work or school. But people with BD have huge mood changes. These mood changes affect their daily lives. They keep people from doing everyday tasks. People find it hard to function. They often have trouble taking care of themselves and their families.

WHAT IS A MOOD EPISODE?

A mood is more than just how a person feels. It also includes the person's energy level and health. Moods shape how people view themselves and others. People with BD have periods of strong emotions.

These are called mood episodes. An episode usually lasts one to two weeks. A person's thoughts, feelings, and actions change during an episode.

"Bipolar" means that there are two extremes. People with BD have two main types of mood episodes. They are manic and depressive episodes. During a manic episode, a person is wildly energetic. This is called mania. Mania can be dangerous. In this state, people are bursting with plans. It is hard for them to calm down or sleep.

Mania makes people feel confident. They may think they can accomplish anything.

They may not be able to control their thoughts and actions. They may do risky things. For example, they might drive fast. They do not think about the danger.

During depressive episodes, people feel sad and hopeless. They are very tired. This feeling is called **depression**. Even simple

---

BIPOLAR DISORDER IN THE ANCIENT WORLD

Doctors in the ancient world did not use the term "bipolar disorder." But they described its symptoms. Hippocrates was a doctor in ancient Greece. He lived from 460 to 375 BCE. He described patients who spoke quickly. Sometimes they got very angry. They even became violent. He called this condition "mania." Hippocrates was the first doctor to describe mania in detail.

tasks seem hard to do. Depression affects people's sleep patterns. People may sleep a lot. Or they may not get enough sleep. Getting out of bed seems impossible. People may avoid family and friends. A depressive episode may last for a long time.

Sometimes people with BD seem fine in between episodes. Some people have mood episodes only once in a while. Others have them many times each year. A mood episode may last for only a few hours or days. But it could last for weeks or months.

Mary Phillips is a scientist. She scans the brains of people with BD. She studies these

During a depressive episode, people feel exhausted and unmotivated. They may also have low self-esteem.

scans to understand how BD affects the brain. She explains, "It's not just that people are high. They are also very low."[3]

There is no cure for BD. The symptoms might go away for a time. But the illness is still there. More mood episodes could

happen in the future.

TYPES OF BIPOLAR DISORDER

There are four types of BD. One type is

called bipolar I. Someone with this type has

manic episodes. Each manic episode may

NAMING BIPOLAR DISORDER

Emil Kraepelin was a German doctor. He lived in the late 1800s. He thought mania and depression were part of the same disease. He called it "manic depressive illness." Other doctors disagreed with Kraepelin. His ideas did not catch on until the 1960s. In 1980, the American Psychiatric Association (APA) started using a different term. It called the condition "bipolar disorder." The APA thought the word *manic* was too similar to *maniac*. The word *maniac* has a negative meaning.

last for seven days or more. The depressive episodes are even longer. A person's depressive episodes may last two weeks or more.

People with bipolar I may not be able to think clearly. They might take dangerous risks during a manic episode. They might try to hurt themselves during a depressive episode.

Another type of BD is called bipolar II. This is the most common type. Depressive episode symptoms in bipolar II are usually worse than in bipolar I. They also last longer. People with bipolar II do not

During a manic or hypomanic episode, people have racing thoughts. They are easily distracted.

have manic episodes. Instead, they may

experience hypomania. Hypomania is

an energetic mood. It is not as intense

as a manic episode. People are still able

to function. But they may make some

bad choices.

A third type of BD is called cyclothymia. It has shorter mood episodes than the other types. Each episode may last only a few days or weeks. Doctors look for certain signs to diagnose an adult with cyclothymia. The person must have mood episodes for at least two years. During those two years, the person must have symptoms at least half the time. There must not be more than two months between mood episodes. Many people with cyclothymia later develop bipolar I or II.

Some people's experiences do not fit into these categories. But they still have manic and depressive episodes. They are diagnosed with the fourth type of BD. It is called bipolar disorder not otherwise specified. Their mood changes may be caused by drug or alcohol abuse. A medical condition, such as a stroke, could also cause these changes.

WHAT CAUSES BIPOLAR DISORDER?

Experts do not know exactly what causes BD. They have found that brain function plays a role. The brain has **cells** called neurons. These cells send messages to each other. The signals tell the body what to do. For example, some signals tell the heart

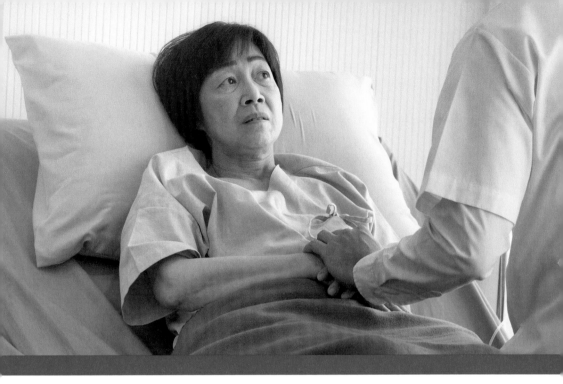

People with BD may need to be hospitalized for health or safety reasons during a mood episode.

to beat. Brain chemicals help neurons pass along information. Dopamine and serotonin are two types of brain chemicals. They help control people's moods. People with BD may have too much of these chemicals. Or they may not have enough. Brain scans show that some areas of the brain are smaller in people with BD. One of these areas processes emotions. Another area helps with planning.

BD often runs in families. Dr. Francis McMahon works for the National Institute of Mental Health. He says, "Bipolar disorder is one of the most strongly inherited mental illnesses."[4] About 85 percent of people with BD have a parent or sibling who also has the disease.

Stressful events can also contribute to BD. A stressful event is one that changes a person's life. The event may be sad, such as the death of a loved one. A happy event could cause **stress** too. For example,

someone may get a promotion at work.

She might worry about doing well in the

new job. Other things can also set off mood

episodes. These include a head injury or the

use of drugs or alcohol.

FAMILY STUDIES

Some people with a family history of BD get the disease. Others do not. Researchers want to know why. They are studying Amish and Mennonite families in Ohio and Pennsylvania. These families live in small communities. Most of the residents share many relatives. This makes it easy for researchers to track families with bipolar disorder. These studies may help doctors learn more about how BD is passed down.

CHAPTER TWO

HOW DOES BIPOLAR DISORDER AFFECT A PERSON'S LIFE?

Each person who has BD experiences it differently. People with BD have cycles. A cycle happens when someone goes through one mania and one depressive episode. Many people have

Mood episodes can vary in length. Episodes can last for days or persist for months at a time.

two cycles per year. But some have four or

more mood episodes in one year. This is

called rapid cycling.

People may feel invincible during a manic episode. They are restless and have a lot of energy.

MANIC EPISODES

During a manic episode, the brain is overactive. People might be jumpy. They are anxious. They react quickly to things. They might speak so quickly that their words run together. They might start many different projects. But they usually do not finish these projects. They cannot focus on things. They go a long time without sleeping. They also have a loss of appetite. They might lose weight. One woman described her manic episodes like this: "You know you need to eat. You haven't eaten in three days. But eating would mean chewing. And you can't chew because you've got things to do."[5]

People usually feel excited and very happy at the start of a manic episode. But then they become irritable. They might yell at their loved ones. They could even become violent.

As the manic episode goes on, some people lose touch with reality. They may hear voices. They may see things that are not really there. Many also develop false beliefs. These beliefs are not based in reality. People in a manic episode believe they can do anything. Melody Moezzi is an author and lawyer. She has BD. During one manic episode, she thought she was a prophet. A prophet is someone who talks to gods. She thought she could not be harmed. So she did dangerous things. She says, "I was crossing streets without looking both ways. Because prophets shouldn't

MARY TODD LINCOLN

Mary Todd Lincoln was the wife of President Abraham Lincoln. She lived in the 1800s. Doctors did not know about BD then. But some experts today think she may have had this disorder. She spent too much money. She was often nervous and got excited easily. President Lincoln was killed in 1865. Mary Todd mourned his death for a long time. She entered a mental hospital in 1875.

have to look both ways when they cross the street, right? Eventually, it got to the point where I thought I could fly."[6]

About half of people with BD experience extreme symptoms like these. In these cases, people may put themselves in danger. They must stay in a hospital for their own safety.

HYPOMANIA

Some people with BD experience hypomania. Their symptoms are not as extreme as the symptoms of a manic episode. These people feel very good. They are active and have lots of plans.

During a manic episode, people may do things without thinking of the consequences, such as quitting a job.

They may start many different projects.

The hypomania lasts at least four days in a

row. But hypomania is less extreme than a

manic episode. People do not lose touch

Bipolar II may be tied to the seasons. Depressive episodes are more likely in the fall and winter.

with reality. Friends and family might not even notice the change in their behavior. But many people who have hypomania still need treatment. This is because they may also have intense depressive episodes.

DEPRESSIVE EPISODES

Depressive episodes also affect people's ability to function. Some people describe feeling empty during these episodes. They may sleep too much. Or they may find it hard to sleep. The activities they normally enjoy doing are no longer fun. They may not want to eat. Or they may eat too much. Their body may feel too heavy to move.

Depressive episodes usually last for one to two weeks. But they can last much longer. One woman had a depressive episode that lasted three years. She said, "It just drains you."[7]

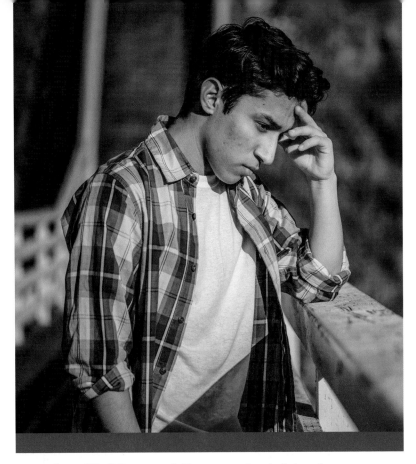

People with BD are at the greatest risk of hurting themselves when they are in a mixed state episode.

People's attitudes change during a depressive episode. They may feel worthless and hopeless. They may think about death a lot. They may even try to kill themselves.

MIXED STATES

People may experience manic and depressive episodes separately. One mood episode may follow right after another. One woman with BD described her experience. She said, "You enjoy the climb up a roller coaster so much that you go off into the clouds and remain there until your thoughts come back to reality. But then, you fall from the clouds into a deep, dark hole."[8]

Sometimes people experience both types of episodes at the same time. This is called a mixed state. People may feel hopeless during a mixed state. But they also have a lot of energy. They feel restless.

Many people with BD say that mixed states

are the worst part of their illness. People in

mixed states often must go to a hospital.

Their intense moods may cause them to

hurt themselves or others.

HOW DO DOCTORS DIAGNOSE BIPOLAR DISORDER?

Most people with BD are diagnosed as

young adults. Doctors observe patients to

learn about their symptoms. They ask the

patients questions about their daily lives.

They may also ask the patients to keep a

record of their activities and moods.

Many people with BD do not realize how bad their symptoms are. For this reason, they do not seek treatment right away. Most people are diagnosed five to ten years after their first mood episode.

People with BD often do not seek help during a manic episode. This is because

CHILDREN AND TEENS

Children and teens can develop BD. The disease is usually worse if it starts at a young age. Young people often have shorter mood episodes. But they may have many episodes in one day. They may alternate quickly between mania and depression. They often struggle in school. They may have a hard time getting along with others. They might even try to hurt themselves.

they feel good during these episodes.

People are most likely to seek help during

a depressive episode. About 60 percent

of these people are wrongly diagnosed

with major depressive disorder (MDD). This

is another type of mood disorder. People

with MDD experience only depressive

episodes. They do not experience mania

or hypomania. People with BD may not

think their mania is a problem. They may

not talk about their mania. Doctors may not

realize that they have manic episodes too.

Or people with BD may not yet have had a

manic or hypomanic episode.

Children or teenagers must have mood episodes for at least one year to be diagnosed with BD.

Treatment is important. Without it, BD can cause many problems. These problems may affect a person's relationships. They can also affect a person's ability to work or go to school.

CHAPTER THREE

HOW DOES BIPOLAR DISORDER AFFECT SOCIETY?

Nearly five percent of the world's population experiences BD during their lifetime. More than 5 million Americans have BD. BD affects equal numbers of men and women. But men and women often

When mood symptoms are severe, it can be difficult for people with BD to take care of themselves.

have different BD symptoms. Women are

more likely to be diagnosed with bipolar II.

About 83 percent of people with BD

have severe symptoms. In these cases, BD

may be a disability. A disability is something

Some employers offer employee assistance programs, which can help people with mental illnesses find treatment options.

that keeps someone from doing everyday activities. BD is covered by the Americans with Disabilities Act (ADA). The ADA protects people with disabilities. Employers must understand how the disability affects a person's work. People with BD may not be able to work full-time. Their employers help them figure out a different work schedule. People with BD may work part-time instead. But they still get work benefits.

WHAT ARE THE FINANCIAL COSTS?

BD can affect people's work and family life. It can make it difficult for people to do their jobs. They may have to take time off from work to recover. Then they can lose money. They might even lose their jobs.

Health care is expensive. This is especially the case for people with BD. They often have to receive long-term treatment. This treatment comes with a cost.

Over their lifetimes, they pay about four times more for health care than people who do not have BD. A lifetime of BD treatment can cost as much as $625,000.

WHAT ARE THE EMOTIONAL COSTS?

People may make hurtful or dangerous choices during mood episodes. This can

EXTREME SPENDING

People may make bad decisions about money when they are manic. They might gamble or go on a shopping spree. Or they might try to start a new business. Most of their money might be gone after the episode is over. They might not be able to care for themselves or their families. This spending can damage people's relationships.

make it hard for friends and family to trust the person. Kay Redfield Jamison is a psychologist. She treats people who have mood disorders. She also has BD. She says, "It took me far too long to realize that lost years and relationships cannot be recovered. That damage done to oneself and others cannot always be put right again."[9]

BD is a lifelong illness. But symptoms usually go away between mood episodes. Other people might think this means that the person is cured. When an episode happens again, they might think the person did something to make the illness come

back. So they blame the person for his

illness. This might make him feel ashamed.

He might avoid going to the doctor because

of these feelings. Feelings of shame can set

off a depressive episode. Many people turn

BIPOLAR DISORDER AND CREATIVITY

BD is common among creative people. This includes artists, writers, and musicians. People have many thoughts during manic episodes. Their minds are overactive. They feel more confident. This can open them up to new ideas. It can also help them connect ideas in new ways. But BD can also hinder the creative process. Artists with BD may not be productive when they have a mood episode. Their work may suffer.

to drugs or alcohol at these times. Others may try to kill themselves.

OTHER HEALTH RISKS

Many people with BD have other mental illnesses as well. Anxiety disorders are common among people with BD. These disorders cause intense fear and worry. People worry about everyday things.

About 60 percent of people with BD use drugs or alcohol. Some people do this to try to manage their moods. People with BD are more prone to developing addictions. Using substances is a risk-taking behavior. People in manic episodes tend to take risks.

So they may start using drugs or alcohol.
Others may use these substances when
they are depressed. They do this to
try to feel better or forget about their
depression. These substances can damage
people's bodies.

Many people with BD have eating
disorders (EDs). Their eating behaviors are
unhealthy. There are many types of EDs.
Some people eat too little food. Others
suffer from bulimia.

More than 45 percent of people with BD
try to kill themselves. This usually happens
during a depressive episode. Often the

Drugs and alcohol can make BD symptoms worse.

person is also using drugs or alcohol. These substances can increase suicidal thoughts.

People with BD face a high risk of death from many different causes. BD affects the brain as well as the rest of the body. People with BD are prone to heart disease. They are also more likely to develop diabetes.

DISORDERS RELATED TO BD

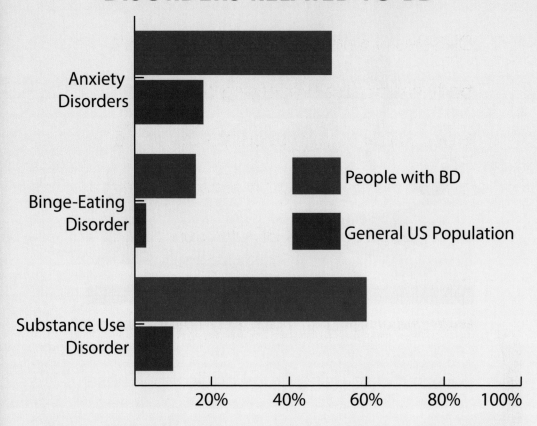

This chart shows some of the most common disorders among people with BD. It also shows how common these disorders are in the general population.

Sources:

Doron Sagman and Mauricio Tohen, "Comorbidity in Bipolar Disorder," Psychiatric Times, March 24, 2009. www.psychiatrictimes.com.

"Facts and Statistics," Anxiety and Depression Association of America, 2018. www.adaa.org.

"10 Percent of US Adults Have Drug Use Disorder at Some Point in Their Lives," National Institutes of Health, November 18, 2015. www.nih.gov.

Tori Rodriguez, "Clinician Insight: Exploring the Link Between Bipolar Disorder and Binge Eating Disorder," Psychiatry Advisor, April 16, 2018. www.psychiatryadvisor.com.

Diabetes is a health condition. A person's body has trouble processing glucose. Glucose is a sugar that comes from food. It helps the body function. Scientists are not sure why people with BD are more prone to these problems.

ACTRESS CARRIE FISHER

Carrie Fisher played Princess Leia in the Star Wars movies. She had bipolar I. She also struggled with drug addiction. She spoke and wrote about her experiences. She said, "I get a feeling like my mind's been having a party all night long and . . . I have to clean up the mess." Fisher educated people about BD. She died from a heart attack in 2016 at the age of sixty.

Quoted in Nikki Finke, "Carrie Fisher: Over the Edge and Back," Los Angeles Times, *July 31, 1987.*
www.latimes.com.

CHAPTER FOUR

HOW CAN BIPOLAR DISORDER BE TREATED?

There are many successful treatments for BD. Mental health professionals treat people with BD. Doctors and psychiatrists are types of mental health professionals. They can **prescribe** medication. During a mood episode, they

Group therapy or support groups can help people who have BD.

try to bring the person's mood back to

normal. The goal of treatment is to relieve

people's symptoms. Another goal is to

prevent future mood episodes.

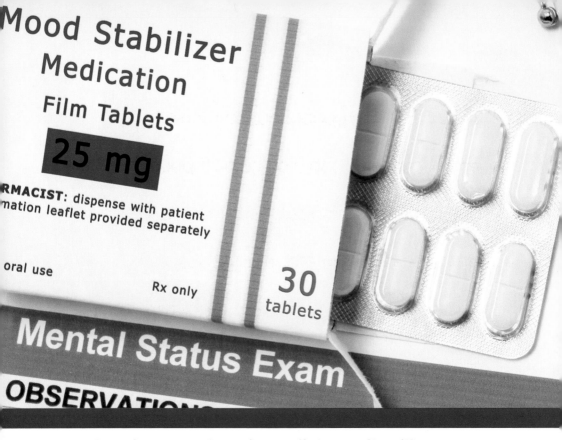

People may not see immediate results with medication. It may take several days for mood stabilizers to take effect.

MEDICATION

Most people with BD take mood stabilizers.

This is a type of medication. To stabilize

something means to make it steady. Mood

stabilizers do this with people's moods.

They can calm people during manic episodes. They can also help lift people out of depressive episodes. This medication can prevent future mood episodes.

The most common mood stabilizer is lithium. It works for most people with BD. Another group of mood stabilizers is anticonvulsants. This medication was originally used to treat **seizures**. A seizure happens when there is a lot of electrical activity in the brain. This may make the person shake uncontrollably. People with BD do not usually have seizures. But their brains become overactive during manic episodes. Anticonvulsants help reduce their brain activity.

Other medications can also help people who have BD. Some people have severe mania. They see or hear things that are not there. They may take antipsychotics. This medication helps manage the mania.

LITHIUM

Lithium is a metal. It is found in rocks and seawater. In the late 1940s, John Cade was experimenting. Cade was an Australian doctor. He found that lithium calmed mania. But it can damage people's organs if they take too much of it. Patients who take lithium must get blood tests often. This is to make sure they have safe levels of lithium in their blood.

Some people with BD are prescribed antidepressants. This type of medication can help people during depressive episodes. It balances the chemicals in people's brains. It may help people feel less hopeless. People with MDD take a different type of antidepressant. This type does not work for people with BD. It can **trigger** a manic episode. So it is important for people to receive the correct diagnosis.

THERAPY

Most people with BD also go to therapy. They meet with a therapist. A therapist is a mental health professional. They are trained

Doctors check in with patients to see whether their medication is working.

to help people who have mental illnesses.

Therapy helps people with BD learn how to

manage their illness.

Cognitive behavioral therapy (CBT) can

help people who have BD. CBT helps

people change their thoughts. People with

BD often have negative thought patterns.

For example, they might feel unwanted. They might think, "No one wants me around." This thought could lead to a depressive episode. CBT helps people focus on positive thoughts instead. This can reduce people's symptoms.

People with BD may also try Interpersonal and Social Rhythm Therapy (ISRT). ISRT focuses on getting enough sleep. A lack of sleep can trigger manic episodes. An ISRT therapist helps people set up daily routines. For example, people may set schedules that they stick to for eating meals. They may go to bed every

During therapy, people with BD learn how to ask for help from friends and family.

night at a certain time. Routines can help

keep people healthy and stable.

Family therapy can also be helpful.

Family members attend therapy sessions

with the patient. People with BD may do

hurtful things during mood episodes. Their

behavior can strain their relationships.

Family therapy gives family members a chance to talk about their feelings. It also helps them learn how to help their loved one.

There are also support groups for people with BD. In a support group, people come together to talk about their experiences. This can help people realize that they are not alone. People can learn from others who have similar struggles.

MEDICAL PROCEDURES

Sometimes medication and therapy are not enough. In this case, a doctor may suggest a medical procedure. This is a medical treatment or operation. It is done in a hospital or doctor's office. The most common medical procedure for BD is electroconvulsive therapy (ECT). ECT can stop a severe mood episode. The doctor gives the patient medicine. The medicine puts the person to sleep. The doctor puts small metal discs on the person's scalp. These are called electrodes. They are connected to wires. The wires send a mild electrical pulse to the brain. This helps the neurons connect to each other better. It can also help new neurons grow. This allows the person's mood to return to normal.

ECT treatment lasts one month. Patients usually receive six to twelve ECT treatments. Then they go back to medication.

ECT helps more than 80 percent of patients. It is most helpful during depressive episodes. But there are side effects. People may have some memory loss after ECT.

VAGUS NERVE STIMULATION

Another type of medical procedure is vagus nerve stimulation (VNS). It is not a common treatment. But it may help when other treatments do not work. Doctors implant a device into a patient's chest. The device sends electrical signals. The signals go to the vagus nerve. This nerve starts at the base of the brain. The signals stabilize the person's mood.

Actress Carrie Fisher wrote about her struggles with BD in some of her memoirs and novels.

Actress Carrie Fisher had BD. She shared

her experiences with ECT. She said,

"Some of my memories will never return.

They are lost—along with the crippling

feeling of defeat and hopelessness. Not a

tremendous price to pay when you think about it."[10]

Transcranial magnetic stimulation (TMS) is another procedure. It can help people who have BD. A doctor holds a magnetic coil against a person's scalp. Electric currents flow through the coil to neurons nearby. TMS helps the neurons connect and grow. It can be done while the patient is awake.

LIFESTYLE CHANGES

Treatment for BD varies from person to person. Each person needs a different mix of treatments. Most people also need to make lifestyle changes. This helps them manage the disease. One of the most important things is to get a healthy amount of sleep. This allows people's mood to reset each day. Exercising often and eating well also help protect the body and brain against other health risks. Keeping up regular daily routines can help prevent mood episodes. Staying connected with other people is also important. It is easy to slip into a mood episode when people avoid family and friends. Alcohol and drugs can also trigger mood episodes. They could interact with medications as well. This could cause

Meditation may help relieve some symptoms of BD. People sit quietly and focus on their breathing.

sickness or even death. People with BD

should avoid these substances.

People with BD need to manage their

stress. They might change their work

schedules. Or they may need to change

jobs. They can ask others for help when

they are busy. Therapists can help them find ways to cope with stress. This can bring down their stress levels. It can help prevent a mood episode.

Many people with BD keep a daily log. They record their moods. They track their sleep. This helps doctors figure out which treatments are working. The log may also show the warning signs of a mood episode. For example, sleeping too much may be a sign of a depressive episode. People can do things to ease the depression. They can reach out to a doctor. They might spend time with loved ones.

BD affects every part of a person's life.

But a person is much more than a disease.

With the right support and treatment,

someone with BD can still have a full and

happy life.

WRITING ABOUT BIPOLAR DISORDER

Heidi Heilig is an author. She writes fantasy novels for teens. She has BD. Some of her characters do too. Her book *For a Muse of Fire* is about a character named Jetta. Jetta has BD. She goes through a long underground tunnel. She has a depressive episode. The tunnel represents what depression feels like. Heilig says, "I want people to . . . root for a character who has bipolar disorder."

Quoted in "Interview with Heidi Heilig, Author of For a Muse of Fire," YA Shelf, October 29, 2018. www.yash3lf.com.

GLOSSARY

cells

the building blocks of all living things that help them function and grow

depression

an intense feeling of hopelessness and sadness that lasts a long time

diagnosed

to have identified an illness or condition based on its symptoms

disorder

a physical or mental condition that affects a person's ability to function and causes distress

prescribe

to write a prescription, or an official recommendation that tells someone which medication to take

seizures

sudden increases in electrical activity in the brain that can cause someone to shake uncontrollably

stress

a feeling of pressure or tension

trigger

to cause or set in motion

SOURCE NOTES

INTRODUCTION: A LIFE OF UPS AND DOWNS

1. Quoted in "Demi Lovato: Simply Complicated," *Phillymack Productions*, 2017. www.youtube.com.

2. Quoted in Suzannah Weiss, "Demi Lovato Explains Why You Shouldn't Call Her Bipolar," *Teen Vogue*, August 27, 2017. www.teenvogue.com.

CHAPTER ONE: WHAT IS BIPOLAR DISORDER?

3. Quoted in "Ride the Tiger: A Guide Through the Bipolar Brain," *PBS*, 2016. www.pbs.org.

4. Quoted in "Large Families May Hold Answers to Bipolar Disorder," *NIH Medline Plus Magazine*, n.d. www.magazine.medlineplus.gov.

CHAPTER TWO: HOW DOES BIPOLAR DISORDER AFFECT A PERSON'S LIFE?

5. Quoted in "Ride the Tiger: A Guide Through the Bipolar Brain."

6. Quoted in "Ride the Tiger: A Guide Through the Bipolar Brain."

7. Quoted in "Ride the Tiger: A Guide Through the Bipolar Brain."

8. Quoted in "Life on a Roller Coaster: Managing Bipolar Disorder," *NIH Medline Plus Magazine*, n.d. www.magazine.medlineplus.gov.

CHAPTER THREE: HOW DOES BIPOLAR DISORDER AFFECT SOCIETY?

9. Quoted in Laura Gold, "Jamison Reflects on Life With 'An Unquiet Mind,'" *Cornell Chronicle*, September 24, 2017. www.news.cornell.edu.

CHAPTER FOUR: HOW CAN BIPOLAR DISORDER BE TREATED?

10. Carrie Fisher, *Wishful Drinking*. New York: Simon and Schuster, 2008. p. 11.

FOR FURTHER RESEARCH

BOOKS

Hilary W. Poole, *Bipolar Disorder*. New York: AV2 by Weigl, 2018.

Richard Spilsbury, *Bipolar Disorder*. New York: Rosen Publishing, 2019.

Richard Spilsbury, *Depression*. New York: Rosen Publishing, 2019.

INTERNET SOURCES

"Bipolar Disorder," *National Institute of Mental Health*, January 2020. www.nimh.nih.gov.

"Bipolar Disorder," *TeensHealth from Nemours*, September 2015. www.kidshealth.org.

"Understanding Your Mood: An Introduction to Depression and Bipolar Disorder," *Depression and Bipolar Support Alliance*, 2017. www.dbsalliance.org.

WEBSITES

bpHope
www.bphope.com

This is *bp Magazine*'s website and blog. The site provides resources and information for people with bipolar disorder.

International Bipolar Foundation
www.ibpf.org

This site shares information about the symptoms and treatment of bipolar disorder.

International Society for Bipolar Disorders
www.isbd.org

This site shares the latest research on bipolar disorder.

The US National Library of Medicine
www.medlineplus.gov

This site has information on many mental health topics, including bipolar disorder.

INDEX

IMAGE CREDITS

ABOUT THE AUTHOR

Kathy MacMillan is a writer, American Sign Language interpreter, librarian, and signing storyteller. She has published seventeen books. She writes picture books, nonfiction for children and adults, and fantasy novels for teens. She is the coauthor of *She Spoke: 14 Women Who Raised Their Voices and Changed the World*. She lives near Baltimore, Maryland, with her kid and three very regal cats.